Life in the Ancient World

Religion in
the Ancient World

Crabtree Publishing Company

www.crabtreebooks.com

Life in the Ancient World

Contributing authors: Paul Challen, Shipa Mehta-Jones,
  Lynn Peppas, Hazel Richardson
Publishing plan research and development:
  Sean Charlebois, Reagan Miller
  Crabtree Publishing Company
Editors: Kathy Middleton, Adrianna Morganelli
Proofreaders: Kathy Middleton, Marissa Furry
Editorial director: Kathy Middleton
Photo research: Katherine Berti, Crystal Sikkens
Designer and prepress technician: Katherine Berti
Print and production coordinator: Katherine Berti

Cover description: Gods and goddesses were represented in
various statues and sculptures such as the statue of Indian hindu
god, Shiva Nataraja (top center), Roman goddess, Ceres (center
left), and Egyptian deity, Bes (bottom center). The Soninke people
of ancient Ghana, in western Africa, used brass masks (top right)
in various religious ceremonies. (bottom right) The introduction of
Christianity to many ancient cultures changed the course of their
histories. (back center) The Parthenon was a temple built by the
ancient Greeks for their goddess Athena.

Title page description: Buddhism is a religion and philosophy
based on teachings of Siddhartha Gautama, who became known
as the Buddha.

Photographs and reproductions:
Art Archive/Museo del Oro Lima/Dagli Orti: page 21 (top)
Erich Lessing/Art Resource, NY: page 29 (bottom)
Private Collection/Bridgeman Art Library: cover (top right)
Corbis: David Lees: page 9 (left); Michael S. Yamashita: page 9
  (right); © Arte & Immagini srl: page 24 (left)
Corel: title page
© J.M. Kenoyer, Courtesy Dept. of Archaeology and Museums,
  Govt. of Pakistan: page 10
Courtesy of National Land Image Information (Color Aerial
  Photographs), Ministry of Land, Infrastructure, Transport and
  Tourism: page 27 (right)
Wikimedia Commons: Reiji Yamashina: 6 (right); Fanghong: page 7
  (top right); Hardnfast: pages 8–9; Bibi Saint-Pol: page 12; Bjørn
  Christian Tørrissen: page 14 (inset); Keith Schengili-Roberts: 15
  (top); David Liam Moran: page 16 (right); Ptcamn: page 18;
  Lamré: page 26 (top); World Imaging: 27 (left), 28 (bottom);
  Ogmios: page 28 (top); Owen Cook: page 28 (middle); Berig
  Badekunda: 31 (top); Laurascudder: page 31 (bottom right)
All other images by Shutterstock.com

Illustrations:
Rose Gowsell: page 23
William Band: pages 22–23, 30

Library and Archives Canada Cataloguing in Publication

CIP available at Library and Archives Canada

Library of Congress Cataloging-in-Publication Data

Religion in the ancient world.
     p. cm. -- (Life in the ancient world)
   Includes index.
   ISBN 978-0-7787-1735-5 (reinforced library binding : alk. paper) -- ISBN 978-0-
7787-1742-3 (pbk. : alk. paper) -- ISBN 978-1-4271-8801-4 (electronic pdf) -- ISBN
978-1-4271-9642-2 (electronic html)
   1. Religions--Juvenile literature. 2. Civilization, Ancient--Juvenile literature.
I. Crabtree Publishing Company.
   BL96.R43 2012
   200.93--dc23
                                                                 2011029256

Crabtree Publishing Company
www.crabtreebooks.com   1-800-387-7650

Printed in Canada/082011/MA20110714

Published in Canada
Crabtree Publishing
616 Welland Ave.
St. Catharines, Ontario
L2M 5V6

Published in the United States
Crabtree Publishing
PMB 59051
350 Fifth Avenue, 59th Floor
New York, New York 10118

Published in the United Kingdom
Crabtree Publishing
Maritime House
Basin Road North, Hove
BN41 1WR

Published in Australia
Crabtree Publishing
3 Charles Street
Coburg North
VIC, 3058

Contents

Religion in the Ancient World

Most historians agree that a civilization is a group of people that shares common languages, some form of writing, advanced technology and science, and systems of government and religion. Each ancient civilization developed these features differently, including its own religion. Influences such as geography, tradition and legends, and trade all had an effect on how each civilization established its beliefs and values.

Worshiping gods

The worship of gods and goddesses was integral to the religions of many ancient civilizations. People believed that pleasing the gods would protect them from natural disasters, sickness and death, and would ensure good crops. They honored the gods through prayer, religious ceremonies and festivals, and **sacrifices**. Over time, trade among civilizations increased, and war and travel resulted in the different cultures of many nations to be introduced to one another. The religions of each ancient civilization became affected, and many people converted, or changed, their religions, and adopted new religious practices.

In ancient Japan, Shinto shrines had a **torii** *gate, sometimes painted orange, at the entrance to the complex. Often, two stone lions would stand guard on either side of the entrance.*

Maps and Timeline of Ancient Civilizations

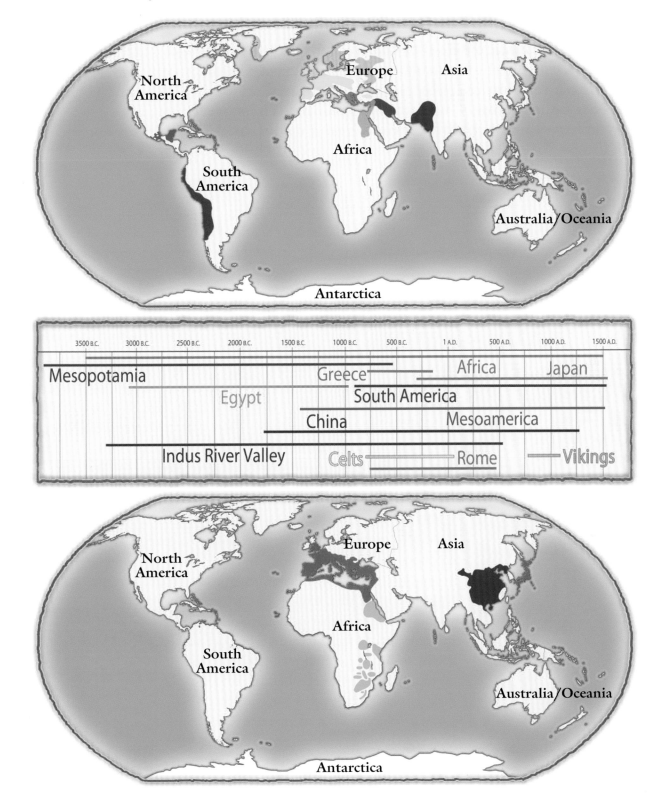

The period described as ancient history is usually defined as the time from first recorded history up to the Early Middle Ages, around 300 A.D. Some of the civilizations in this book begin well after the ancient period but are included because they were dominant early civilizations in their regions. The beginning and ending dates of early civilizations are often subject to debate. For the purposes of this book, the timelines begin with the first significant culture in a civilization and end with the change or disappearance of the civilization. The end was sometimes marked by an event such as invasion by another civilization, or simply by the gradual dispersion of people due to natural phenomena such as famine or earthquakes.

Ancient China

1766 B.C.–1271 A.D.

As China expanded trade outside its borders with other countries, new religious ideas from other cultures spread across China. Ancient Chinese religion and philosophy were based around four different belief systems, or ways of thinking. These were ancestor **worship, Taoism, Confucianism, and Buddhism. Most ancient Chinese followed ideas contained in one of these systems.**

Sons of Heaven

The ancient Chinese people called their emperors "Sons of Heaven," because they believed the leaders were chosen by the gods. Emperors were expected to act in the best interest of the Chinese people. The Chinese believed that their ancestors in heaven brought prosperity and protection to them when an emperor was fair and just. If an emperor acted badly, or was a poor military leader, the heavenly ancestors were thought to show their displeasure by sending earthquakes, floods, and droughts. The people took the natural disasters as a sign to rebel and replace the emperor. The Chinese people called this the Mandate of Heaven.

Ancestor Worship

Family was at the center of ancient Chinese society. Family included all current relatives, ancestors from the past, as well as from future generations. Respect for past generations was so important that many people prayed to the spirits of their ancestors for help and guidance. In most ancient Chinese homes there was an **altar** where offerings could be made to dead relatives. The family name was very important to the ancient Chinese. The family name was carried on only through the male members of the family, so people felt it was important to have sons as heirs.

Confucianism

Confucius was a scholar who lived from 551 B.C. to 479 B.C. Confucius was born into a wealthy family, but war caused his family to become poor. To improve himself, Confucius began to study. He became one of the wisest men in China. Confucius developed a system of rules of behavior. The rules stated that sons owed loyalty to fathers, wives owed loyalty to husbands, and younger brothers owed loyalty to older brothers. Confucius believed that if these rules were followed, Chinese society would be more peaceful. Just as a father was responsible for caring for his family, Confucius believed the emperor was responsible for treating his subjects wisely and fairly. Confucius thought children should obey their elders and the Chinese people should obey their emperor.

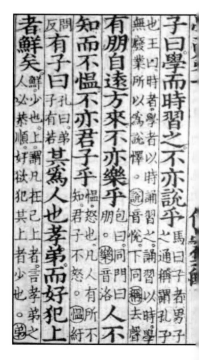

Confucius (left) was known as The Master. His teachings are in a book called The Analects *(right).*

The Leshan Buddha was carved out of a cliff face in Sichuan province during the Tang Dynasty (618–907 A.D.)

The White Horse Temple is thought to be the first Buddhist temple in China.

Buddhism

Buddhism is based on the teachings of Siddhartha Gautama, who became known as the Buddha, or "Enlightened One." Gautama became saddened by the suffering in the world and decided to go on a journey from his home in India. Gautama felt that he had found the meaning of life after **meditating** near a tree. Followers of Buddha, called Buddhists, believe that people suffer because they want things and they will only be happy once they stop wanting things. Buddhism spread through China between 1 A.D. and 100 A.D.

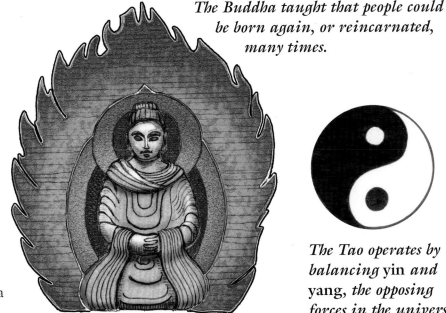

The Buddha taught that people could be born again, or reincarnated, many times.

The Tao operates by balancing yin *and* yang, *the opposing forces in the universe.*

Taoism

Between 600 and 500 B.C., a way of thinking known as Taoism developed in China. Taoism is based on the *Tao Te Ching,* a book written by a teacher named Lao Tzu. Lao Tzu taught the importance of harmony with nature and that achieving a balance of the forces of *yin* and *yang* is the key to spiritual peace. Lao Tzu created Taoism to end the constant fighting in Chinese society. Tzu believed fighting was a sign that *yin* and y*ang* were out of balance. In 440 A.D., the emperor declared Taoism a national religion. From then on, Lao Tzu was honored as a god.

A stone sculpture stands near the city of Quanzhou, China, honoring Lao Tzu, the founder of Taoism.

Ancient Mesopotamia

Mesopotamia is the name given to the region, now in modern-day Iraq, where many different peoples made their homes, including the Sumerians, Akkadians, and Assyrians. Religion, or the relationship between people and the gods and goddesses they worshiped, was a central part of life in Mesopotamia. The temple was at the heart of a city-state, **and was a storehouse for the city's wealth, knowledge, and leadership. Religion was passed from generation to generation, through myths and legends about the gods and goddesses and through the traditions and duties that were held** sacred **in the temple.**

Gods and Goddesses

The first gods worshiped in the region were believed to be in control of natural forces. The goddess of love and war was called Ishtar, or Inanna. Over time, Mesopotamians came to believe that their gods had human characteristics and would look after their city-states if they were honored in certain ways. In later Mesopotamian times, gods and goddesses were called upon by people for help and guidance. People believed that failure to honor the gods brought floods, droughts, disease, and attacks from enemies. The Mesopotamians believed that harmful spirits existed all around them, especially in deserts and ruins. These spirits rode on the wind or floated on the water, but they were not clever and could easily be deceived. People prayed to their gods for protection against evil spirits.

Homes for the Gods

Temples, which were called the houses of the gods or goddesses, were a central feature of Mesopotamian cities. Each city had a protector **deity** whose temple was the largest and most prominent. Temples were part of larger complexes that included residences for priests, schools for **scribes**, workshops for craftspeople, and storehouses for goods. Some temples also had a ziggurat, a stepped pyramid with a shrine on top, attached to them. The ziggurat was used to celebrate the New Year's festival to guarantee the **fertility** of the land.

Priests

Priests had special power in the community. The primary duty of priests was to honor the gods, but different groups of priests conducted different types of temple business. High priests read **omens** and advised kings. Other priests performed magic and rituals and told fortunes. Priests were also believed to have the ability to trap evil spirits and transfer them to other animals. Priestesses, who were women, also served the gods and goddesses. Schools, called *e-dubbas*, developed as priests began training young boys as scribes to read and write **cuneiform**. They studied math, astrology, law, and medicine. To prepare them for life in the priesthood, young boys were taught divining, the art of reading the will of the gods, and of predicting the future.

Large temples usually included a ziggurat, dedicated to the main god or goddess of the city. The remains of the ziggurat from the ancient Sumerian city of Ur are shown below. It is an archaeological site in present-day Iraq. The word ziggurat comes from the Akkadian word zaqaru, *which means "to be high."*

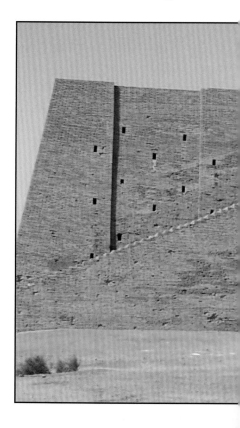

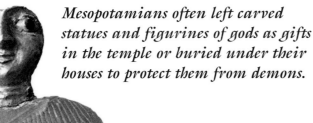

Mesopotamians often left carved statues and figurines of gods as gifts in the temple or buried under their houses to protect them from demons.

In early Sumerian times, priest-kings led the army and acted as go-betweens for people and their gods.

The End of an Age

After the Babylonians defeated Assyria in 614 B.C., Mesopotamia was ruled by a series of Babylonian kings who fought one another for power. There were some parts of the **empire** that were still loyal to Assyria. Babylon's last king was named Nabonidus. The priests of Babylon turned against Nabonidus when he ignored festivals that honored the chief god of the city, Marduk. The priests of Babylon welcomed the invasion of the Persians led by Cyrus the Great in 539 B.C. The Persian army entered the city without a fight, and Babylon became a territory in the Persian empire. By 500 B.C., all of Mesopotamia was controlled by the Persian empire.

Ancient Indus River Valley

Two of the world's greatest ancient civilizations began in the Indus River Valley, in what is now Pakistan—the Harrapans and the Aryans. Archaeologists think the Harappans worshiped many gods. When the Aryans invaded the Indus River Valley, they brought their religion with them. Over the next 1,000 years, the Aryans' religion changed, borrowing beliefs from Harappan and other cultures. Over time, Aryan beliefs developed into the Hindu religion. Other religions also developed in ancient India.

3300 B.C.–550 A.D.

Harappan Beliefs

It is hard to know exactly what the Harappans believed because nobody can understand their form of writing, or **script**. Archaeologists think they worshiped many human and animal gods, as well as tree and river spirits. They also believed in some form of life after death. Harappans put pottery jars in the graves of their dead. The jars contained food to be eaten in the afterlife.

Aryans and the Birth of Hinduism

The Aryans believed that gods, or *devas*, controlled all things in nature, such as weather, fire, and water. They also believed that helper gods created wealth and happiness, healed illnesses, protected roads, and even got people out of bed each morning. One such god was Shiva, Lord of Creatures. Shiva may also have been a Harappan god.

Death and Reincarnation

One of the most important Aryan gods was Agni, the god of fire. Aryans cremated, or burned, their dead, in the belief that Agni carried the souls to the afterlife. Good people went to heaven, while evil people were cast into a pit of blackness. The pit was replaced by a belief in reincarnation, or that every living thing goes through a series of lives. Hindus today do not believe in an afterlife, but they still cremate their dead.

Harappans buried their dead in pits, with the bodies laid out in coffins in a north-south direction, often with tools or simple jewelry.

Sacred Books

The Aryans' holy books, called the Vedas, are a collection of hymns, stories, and rituals. They are a historical record of what life was like 4,000 years ago in India. Aryan boys of the *brahman* caste, or social level, of wealthy families went to school to learn the sacred Vedas from *gurus*. The ancient Indians did not develop a written system of Sanskrit for more than 1,000 years. The Vedas were memorized and passed down from *brahman* to *brahman*. The first known Sanskrit writing is a copy of the Rig Veda holy book written around 400 B.C. The four Veda books, the Rig Veda, Sama Veda, Yajur Veda, and the Atharva Veda are studied by religious scholars, historians and linguists, or people who study and compare languages.

Karma

Hindus believe people are reincarnated, or reborn, after they die. What they are reincarnated as depends on karma, which in turn depends on how that person acted in previous lives. Someone who does good deeds builds up good karma. In the new life, that person may be wealthier or in a higher caste than in the previous life. A person with bad karma is reborn into a low caste, as an animal, or even as a plant. Hindu *brahmans* used the law of karma to explain the caste system. They believed that a person was born a *dasa*, or the lowest level in society, because that person had been bad in a previous life.

Ending the Cycle

The cycle of reincarnation ends only when a person becomes aware of being one with the universe upon death. Release from the cycle can be achieved by devout worship of one of the many Hindu gods.

The Buddha

In 560 B.C., Siddhartha Gautama was born into a wealthy Hindu family. When he was 29 years old, he became aware of suffering, and set out in search of an answer to human misery. For six years, Siddhartha wandered across India, visiting great teachers, or *gurus*. Then, at the age of 35, he spent a night under a tree in meditation. He had visions of his former lives and suddenly understood the cause of misery and cycle of reincarnation. In Siddhartha Gautama's awakening, or enlightenment, he saw no suffering, greed, or hatred. He called this *nirvana*, and believed it was something a person could reach by following a set of eight rules for living which he called the eightfold path. His followers called him the Buddha, or Enlightened One. Buddhism was spread throughout India and the rest of Asia by traveling monks and holy men. Many people adopted the religion because they felt it helped relieve their suffering. The Buddha's teachings developed into a religion that still exists today, 2,500 years after the Buddha was born.

In 260 B.C., Asoka, one of India's most famous rulers, sent his army to conquer the native peoples of southern India. The slaughter that followed horrified Asoka. He began to study the new Indian religion of Buddhism, which said killing is wrong and that all men are equal and deserve respect. He was so impressed with Buddhist ideas that he made Buddhism the official religion of his kingdom. Asoka ordered thousands of stone pillars and *stupas*, or monuments with domed shapes which represent the Buddha, to be raised across India. Laws on how to behave, known as *dharma*, were carved on the stupas.

Jainism

Jainism is a religion based on the idea that people should be truthful, not want too much, and not steal or use violence against other living things. Jains follow the teachings of Vardhamana Mahavira, who lived at the same time as Buddha. Mahavira was a prince who gave up his wealth and traveled around India, meditating and teaching. One of his most important teachings was to not harm other living things, including animals and plants. Today, nearly four million Jains still follow this ancient religion.

*This **stupa**, or stone monument, with a carved pillar gateway was built by the ruler Asoka. He commanded that there be respect for the dignity of all men, religious tolerance, and non-violence.*

Ancient Greece

The ancient Greeks believed that their world was ruled by gods and goddesses. They created myths, or stories about the lives of gods, goddesses, and heroes. Heroes were special human beings descended **from the gods.**

Gods and Goddesses

The ancient Greeks believed that their gods and goddesses looked like muscular men and beautiful women but possessed **supernatural** powers. Gods could use the forces of nature to cause storms at sea, **famine**, or earthquakes. The most important gods and goddesses, such as Zeus, Athena, Poseidon, and Apollo were believd to live on top of Mount Olympus in northern Greece. Zeus, the king of the gods, ruled the sky and the weather. Athena was the goddess of wisdom. Posiedon ruled the sea and was the favorite god of the sailors. Apollo, god of the Sun, crossed the sky each day in his blazing chariot. The god Hades did not live on Mount Olympus but in the underworld where he judged people who died.

Heroic Stories

The Greeks also told stories about special human beings, descended from the gods, called heroes. The stories of these heroes often made points about human weaknesses and strength. Heracles was a great hero who accomplished many tasks that required enormous strength. Theseus was a hero who killed the dreaded Minotaur, a creature that was half man, half bull. Achilles, the greatest of all Greek heroes, defeated Troy's greatest warrior, Hector, during the **Trojan War**.

Religious Rituals and Sacrifice

The ancient Greeks believed that to please the gods they must worship them with elaborate festivals, athletic events, solemn rituals, and sacrifices. People offered the gods incense, flowers, pottery, gold, precious fabric, food, and wine. They believed that the gods also craved blood-sacrifice, so they killed animals, such as bulls, calves, sheep, boar, and pigs. An altar was first sprinkled with wine and barley and then the sacrificial victims were led to the altar where their throats were slit with a small knife or axe.

Religious Festivals

Religious festivals played an important part in ancient Greek life. Athenians celebrated the religious festival of Panathenaia every year. The Panathenaia honored Athena, the **patron** goddess of Athens, and thanked her for protecting the city. During this festival, the best musicians, athletes, and soldiers performed in competitions. A parade of twirling acrobats, singers, and costumed jugglers wound its way through the city to Athena's temple on the Acropolis. A massive statue of Athena was inside the Parthenon, a temple, in the shadowy **sanctuary**. It stood 40 feet (12 meters) tall and its wooden frame was covered with gold and ivory. Outside, at Athena's altar, 100 or more bulls were killed, roasted, and served to everyone. For the poor, the festival of Panathenaia was one of the few times they ate meat.

The Greeks had myths, or stories, about the origin of the Earth, as well as the origin of their gods. This painting depicts the myth of the birth of the goddess Athena. Athena was said to have sprung from Zeus' head in a full suit of armor.

Olympic Games

The ancient Olympic Games began in 776 B.C. in the town of Olympia as part of a religious festival to honor Zeus. The competition included wrestling, boxing, chariot racing, discus and javelin throwing, jumping, and running. The games brought together athletes, who competed naked, from all over Greece. During war, a truce brought a temporary end to fighting until the games were over. Champions were awarded garlands of olive leaves and ribbons to wear on their arms. Every city-state made its winning athletes into heroes and awarded them gifts when they returned home. Women could not compete in the games and married women were forbidden from even watching.

Oracles

Greeks who wanted to learn about what their future held consulted an oracle. An oracle was a god who gave answers to questions through a priestess. The most popular oracle was found at Delphi, where the sun god, Apollo, had a sanctuary. Apollo's advice was sought after by Greeks, foreigners, and even military generals. They all hoped the oracle would give them answers to specific questions, such as whether it was a good time to fight a war. Sometimes the oracle's advice was clear, while at other times it was confusing.

Healing Arts

Sick people in ancient Greece relied on magic charms to cure them. They flocked to shrines to make offerings to the gods, in the hope of getting relief from ailments such as headaches, blindness, and pimples. Ancient Greek doctors healed wounds caused by war and fractures and dislocations common with athletes but they knew very little about disease. Ancient Greek medicine changed with the work of Hippocrates. Born on the island of Kos around 460 B.C., Hippocrates believed that time, not temple sacrifices, cured disease. He also believed that disease came from natural causes, not the actions of the gods. In order to avoid disease, people had to have good hygiene and eat a healthy diet. By considering the facts and then deciding what the sufferer had, Hippocrates predicted how a disease would progress.

Every ancient Greek city had a temple where the people came to worship, or honor, the god or goddess who protected the city. The Parthenon is a temple dedicated to Athena, the goddess whom the people of Athens considered their patron.

Reason for the Seasons

Ancient Greeks explained the weather, earthquakes, and disease with myths. The myth of Demeter and Persephone explains why the seasons change. When the goddess Demeter learned that Hades had kidnapped her daughter, Persephone, and taken the young girl to his underworld home to be his wife, she was filled with grief. When Demeter mourned her loss, nothing grew on the Earth.

It became cold and barren and this was called winter. Zeus sent his messenger, Hermes, to rescue Persephone and return her to her mother. Demeter was so pleased that she brought new growth to the earth and this was called spring. Unfortunately, Persephone had to return to her husband in the underworld for a few months every year but came back to Mount Olympus and her mother every spring, starting the cycle of growth on Earth once again.

Ancient Egypt

For thousands of years, the ancient Egyptians worshiped their pharaoh as a god. Egyptians believed their pharaoh, or king, controlled the weather and the Nile River. They thought he was the only one who could please Hapi, the flood god, and guarantee a supply of water for growing crops. Without the flood, there would be famine. They worshiped other gods and goddesses, too. People believed that everything in life, from the arrival of spring each year to the loss of a lucky amulet, depended entirely on the attitudes of their gods.

Gods and Goddesses

Amun-Re was the supreme god of ancient Egypt. He was also depicted as a sun god. The sun god was honored by all Egyptians because the sun made crops grow and brought life to the world. Other Egyptian gods were worshiped at specific times of the year or in different areas of the country. Some gods looked human, and some looked like animals. The god Harmakhis, or the Sphinx, looked like both. Fearsome traits of animals were associated with the gods' power over people. Thoth, god of learning and wisdom and the inventor of writing, had a human body but the head of an ibis, a bird with a long, slender bill. Hathor, goddess of love, childbirth, music, and dance, had a human form and a pair of cow's horns. Anubis, guardian of tombs, also had a human form but a jackal's head. Jackals were animals that prowled the graveyards, digging up human bones. Egyptians thought jackals knew how to guide and protect the dead on their journey to the afterlife.

Temples and Monuments

Pharaohs built massive temples from stone, where they believed gods and goddesses lived. Gods, like the dead, were thought to have the same needs as living people, including food, cleanliness, rest, and entertainment. Only the pharaoh and his priests and nobles were permitted inside the carved columns of temples to serve the gods or to attend ceremonies. Ordinary Egyptians never went closer than the outer courtyard.

The famous pharaoh Tuthankamen was buried wearing a gold mask. The cobra and vulture emblems on the front of the mask were thought to protect him in the afterlife.

The Temple of Karnak at Luxor was built over a period of several centuries. It was dedicated to the god Amun-Re, the chief god of Egypt, protector of the pharaohs.

The Afterlife

The ancient Egyptians believed that after death, the spirit of a person traveled to heaven where it would live forever. The spirit was given many tests on its journey to the afterlife and the dead were buried with spells and charms to protect them. Mummies were also buried with all of their precious possessions for the afterlife and food for the journey.

Before the journey could begin, the body had to be preserved through a process called mummification. Ancient Egyptians believed the soul left the body at death but it later rejoined the body and stayed throughout eternity. Egyptians mummified their dead to preserve their bodies from decay and to give the soul a home.

After the organs were removed from the body, they were placed in jars.

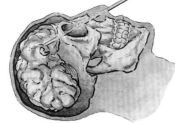

1. It took about 70 days to mummify a body. First, **embalmers** removed the brain through the nose using a special curved hook.

2. Internal organs were removed next, but not the heart. It was believed that intelligence and emotions were contained in the heart, which was needed to pass a test posed by Osiris, god of the underworld, on the way to the afterlife, where they would live again.

3. After the organs were removed, the embalmers covered the body with natron salt, to dry it and prevent decay. The body then rested for 40 days. After 40 days, melted resin, or tree sap, was poured over the shriveled mummy to preserve the skin.

4. Organs that were needed for the afterlife were stored in jars.

5. The body was packed with sand, spices, and scented oil and linen, to give it shape. It took fifteen days to wrap the mummy.

6. During the final stage, a funeral mask was placed over the mummy's face and the mummy was laid to rest in a decorated coffin. Pharaohs and wealthy nobles were placed in pyramids or tombs with items needed in the afterlife including beds and stools, jewelry, clothing, sandals, and chariots.

7. A priest dressed as Anubis, the jackal-headed god of the dead, weighed the heart and the dead person's faults and good deeds.

Anubis was an ancient Egyptian god depicted with the head of a jackal.

Many historians believe that the Pyramids of Giza were built to house the remains of deceased pharaohs.

Ancient Africa

Many cultures co-existed in ancient Africa, including the Egyptians, Nubians, Aksumites, and the peoples of Great Zimbabwe and the western African civilizations. Most ancient Africans worshiped many gods, including a supreme creator god. They also believed in a life after death that was much like life on Earth. Over time, as they came into contact with peoples from other lands, some African civilizations came to accept the beliefs of other religions.

The Spirit World

Cultures throughout ancient Africa believed that every object, alive or not, contained a spirit. They also believed that the spirits of dead ancestors lived on Earth. Both these types of spirits could be angered or pleased by people's actions. Angry spirits were thought to cause bad luck. Religious leaders held ceremonies with singing and dancing to honor the spirits, and people offered food, drink, and other gifts to keep the spirits happy. Many African cultures still hold these beliefs today.

Nubian Burials

In Kerma, the first capital city of the Nubian kingdom of Kush, dead kings were buried in small chambers in the center of huge mounds of earth. Stone models of ships were put around the body in the belief that they would carry the king on the river to the afterlife. Influenced by the Egyptians, the Nubians began to preserve their dead rulers by mummifying them, starting around 900 B.C. They then placed the bodies in pyramids. Nubians who were not rulers were buried in pits. Food and the person's belongings, including pottery jars and tools, which were thought to be needed in the afterlife, were placed around the body. After the burial, the pits were covered with thousands of decorative black and white pebbles.

Shabtis, or statues, were often buried with rulers to server the deceased in the afterlife.

The god Bes was worshiped by both the Nubians and the Egyptians.

16

For more than 600 years, members of the Nubian royal family were buried inside the pyramids at Meroë after their deaths. The pyramids were made of real sandstone.

Masks and Beliefs

Many ancient African civilizations honored the spirits of the dead. Communities held gatherings to watch dancers in masks that resembled their dead ancestors. People offered the dancers gifts of food in order to show their dead ancestors that they had not been forgotten. In ancient Nubia and Egypt, a mask resembling the dead person was placed over the face to help guide the spirit back to the person's body.

First Christian State

The early Aksumites worshiped several gods. Mahrem, protector of kings, was the Aksumites' supreme god. The Aksumites believed that three main gods controlled nature: Beher, the god of the sea; Meder, the goddess of the Earth; and Astar, the god of the heavens. Around 300 A.D., King Ezana of Aksum decided to make his land the world's first Christian state. Christianity was a religion that followed the teachings of Jesus Christ, who followers believed to be the son of God. By about 500 A.D., Christianity was the main religion of all Aksumites. It remained the major religion in what is now Ethiopia, even after the Aksumite civilization collapsed.

The Rise of Islam

Around 900 A.D., traders from Arabia spread the religion of Islam throughout northern and western Africa. Islam was founded by the prophet Muhammad, who was born in 570 A.D., in the Arabian city of Mecca. Muhammad received and spread the teachings of Allah, or God, and they were recorded in a holy book called the Qur'an. Followers of Islam are called Muslims. They believe that Allah is the only god, and that Muhammad was his prophet. Islam also spread through trade to the Swahili Coast in eastern Africa.

The Grand Mosque of Djenne in Mali is the largest mud-brick building in the world.

Ancient Mesoamerica

Ancient Mesoamericans settled in the region between North and South America and worshiped many gods. In a period of 3,000 years, the Olmec, Aztec, Maya, and other peoples such as the Toltec and Zapotec, charted the skies to tell time and built enormous pyramids in which they worshiped their gods. They asked their gods to protect them from danger by making special offerings, called sacrifices. Sacrifices included flowers, vegetables, precious stones, and live animals. The Aztecs believed that they also needed to make bloody human sacrifices to make the gods happy.

1400 B.C.–1521 A.D.

Powerful Kings

Each Olmec, Maya, and Aztec community, or city-state, had a ruler, and each ruler was treated like a god. The Olmec people built city-states with grand pyramid-shaped temples in the center that were used for religious ceremonies. Olmec rulers also served as religious leaders and grew very powerful over the city-states and the surrounding area.

A king ruled each Maya city-state. The Maya believed a king had special powers to communicate with the gods. Maya kings wore elaborate clothing and headdresses representing animals to identify them as gods. Archaeologists have identified a number of the Maya gods by studying the glyphs, or familiar pictures, in three surviving Maya manuscripts called codices.

Flower Wars

Sacrificing prisoners was so important to the Aztecs that the leader and priest Tlacelel organized wars, called Flower Wars, for the sole purpose of capturing warriors to sacrifice to the gods. Flower Wars were planned events, with the best warriors from city-states meeting at an arranged time and place to try to take captives to be sacrificed. The Aztecs believed that the gods needed human blood to protect the universe.

A Bad Omen

The Aztecs used signs they saw in the sky to predict disasters. In 1519, Spanish explorer Hernán Cortés sailed to the coast of Mexico with 500 soldiers in search of gold. A comet appeared just before the Spanish encountered the Aztecs. Aztec emperor Motecuhzoma thought Cortés was the god Quetzalcoatl, whom legend said would one day return. He invited the Spanish leader and his army to rest at his palace. His mistaken belief proved to be the undoing of the Aztec empire. Ill-equipped to defend themselves against the Spanish armies, the Aztecs were defeated in 1521.

Aztec God of War

The Aztec made more sacrifices to Huitzilopochtli, their god of the sun and war, than to any other god. The Aztec believed that to defeat their enemies, they had to sacrifice large numbers of war captives to the god. Tlacaelel, an Aztec military leader, ordered that a large pyramid-temple be erected in Huitzilopochtli's honor. To celebrate the temple's completion, Tlacaelel ordered that more than 80,000 victims be sacrificed!

Blood Sacrifices

1. The Aztecs built a great pyramid 200 feet (50 meters) high in the middle of the city of Tenochtitlán that served as a holy site.

2. Two temples were built on top of the pyramid. One temple was dedicated to Tlaloc, the god of rain. The other was dedicated to Huitzilopochtli, the god of the sun and war. Human sacrifices were performed outside these temples.

3. Human sacrifice victims were usually prisoners captured during battle. Priests held the victim over a flat stone. While the prisoner was still alive, another priest cut open his chest, took his heart out, and held it up to the sky.

4. A ceremonial knife made of obsidian or flint and decorated with jade was used by the priest to cut open the victim. Sometimes hundreds of human sacrifices were made in a day.

5. The dead bodies of sacrificed prisoners were thrown down the 113 steps of the pyramid onto a round stone at the bottom.

Rulers often wore jaguar skins during religious ceremonies as a symbol of their power.

Ancient South America

Many of the ancient South American civilizations—the Chavín, the Moche, the Nazca, and the powerful Incas—developed in the Andes mountains in the present-day country of Peru. The ancient Andeans believed in many gods, and thought that spirits lived in rivers, mountains, and other parts of nature. These early civilizations mummified their dead, built pyramids and temples to make sacrifices to honor their gods, and prayed to the gods for protection from enemies and natural disasters.

900 B.C.–1572 A.D.

Shamans

Shamans were spiritual leaders who performed ceremonies to cure the sick, make **prophecies**, and control volcanic eruptions, floods, and other natural events. Chavín shamans made a powder from a cactus, then inhaled it through hollowed-out animal bones to put themselves into trances. Shamans believed that by doing this, they became jaguars and could perform magic. Moche shamans called on animal spirits to help solve problems, such as defeating enemies and coping with drought, or periods of little rain. They also wore jaguar masks and chanted to the gods for help. Inca shamans drank a tea brewed from bark and plants that made them dream and make prophecies.

Ancient Andean Gods

As early as 2000 B.C., the Andean peoples worshiped a god known as the staff god. Later, both the Chavín and Nazca worshiped this god. He had fangs and claws, and held a staff, or stick. Some historians believe that the Incas adapted the staff god into Viracocha, their god of creation, since images of Viracocha look like the staff god. The Incas believed that Inti, their sun god, was the giver of life.

The Sapa Inca

The ruler, or emperor of the Incas, was called the Sapa Inca. He performed religious ceremonies on special occasions, such as the first plowing of the fields in spring. The Sapa Inca was believed to be descended from the sun god, Inti, and was worshiped by his people as a god. When a Sapa Inca traveled, his face was hidden by fabric because his appearance was thought to be too powerful for humans to see. When a Sapa Inca died, his body was mummified and kept in his palace. During religious festivals, the body was paraded through the streets of Cuzco.

Sacrifices

The ancient Andeans killed humans and animals as sacrifices and offered the bodies to their gods. They believed this would please the gods and prevent earthquakes and other disasters, and also ensure good crops. The Moche sacrificed prisoners of war, removed the flesh from the bodies, and hung the skeletons in their temples. The Incas sacrificed children by burying them alive on mountaintops, where it was believed they would become mountain gods.

Shamans wore jaguar masks when performing religious rituals.

The Afterlife

Ancient burial sites show that the early Andeans believed people continued to live in another world, called the afterlife, after they died. Peasants were wrapped in simple cotton cloth and buried with the tools they would need for working in the afterlife. Graves of rulers were filled with gold and silver utensils, jewelry, pottery jars, and beautiful woven cloth.

The ancient Andeans mummified their dead rulers and nobles. They believed that their rulers were gods who could protect them, even in death. Coastal civilizations, including the Nazca and the Moche, made mummies by drying bodies in the arid desert air. The mountain civilizations, including the Incas, freeze-dried the bodies of their nobles in the cold mountain air. The cold air mummified the bodies, which are called ice mummies. Most of the mummies were buried in a sitting position, wrapped in blankets.

Mummies have been discovered in ancient temples. By examining the mummies, archaeologists have discovered many things about the life of ancient South Americans, including their diet, their clothing, and the diseases they suffered from. The bodies of sacrificed Inca children were so well preserved in the freezing mountain air that scientists have even been able to identify the last meals the children ate.

The Nazca Lines

The Nazca created huge designs on the coastal plains of Peru. They are so big they can only be entirely seen from the air. The Nazca cleared the red surface soil to reveal lighter soil underneath, creating line patterns and images of humans, spiders, monkeys, and birds. They also drew straight lines thousands of feet long. Some of these lines spread outward from a single spot like spokes on a wheel. These patterns are known as ray centers. Some historians believe that the Nazca lines were prayers to the gods for rain. The patterns have survived thousands of years because the dry plains of Peru receive such little rain.

The Inca mummified rulers and nobles, adorning them with gold headdresses and jewelry as a sign of respect and honor.

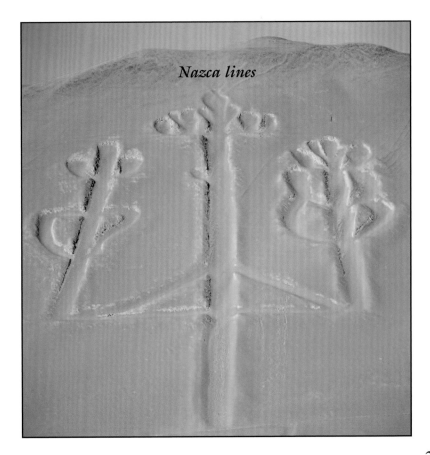

Nazca lines

21

Machu Picchu

Machu Picchu is a city high in the Andes mountains. It was built under the Inca ruler, Pachacuti, around 1460. Some historians believe that the city had religious functions, while others believe that it was built to be Pachacuti's royal summer estate. About 750 people lived there, and most were servants or artisans who worked for the Sapa Inca and the nobles who lived there. Machu Picchu was abandoned when the Spanish arrived in the mid-1500s. Machu Picchu was not found again until 1911.

An Ancient Ceremony

Peruvians continue to hold many traditional ceremonies, such as Qoyllur Riti. Pilgrims climb for five hours to a mountain shrine, as their ancestors did long ago. A shrine at the summit was once dedicated to the *apus*, or gods, of the mountains and hills. Today, the shrine has become an important symbol for Christians, people who follow the teachings of Jesus Christ. This shows how the Spanish, who were Christian, influenced ancient Andean beliefs.

1. The *intihuatana*, a carved stone that may have been used for a sun ceremony, sits on top of a rock at Machu Picchu's highest level.

2. Prayers, sacrifices, and ceremonies honoring the sun were held in the large plaza.

3. The royal compound, housing the Sapa Inca and nobles, was set apart from the other houses.

4. Most buildings and walls in the city were made of granite blocks cut using stone tools, then smoothed with sand. The blocks fit together perfectly without **mortar**.

5. Maize and other crops were grown on the terraces built on the steep mountainside. Stone irrigation canals brought water to the crops.

6. Machu Picchu sits on a ridge between two mountain peaks and is invisible from below. The ridge is located 7,710 feet (2,350 meters) above sea level.

Ancient Rome

The ancient city of Rome spread out over seven hills along the Tiber River in what is now central Italy. Rome grew to become a massive empire that stretched from Britain in the west to North Africa in the south and Asia in the east. Romans worshiped gods and goddesses who they believed controlled different parts of their lives. They created sculptures and temples for these gods and held festivals in their honor.

753 B.C.– 476 A.D.

The Birth of an Empire

According to Roman **mythology**, Mars, the Roman god of war, had twin sons named Romulus and Remus, with his servant. Their uncle, who feared the children would become too powerful, threw them into the Tiber River. The twins were rescued and suckled by a wolf, then raised by a shepherd. When they grew up, each founded a settlement on one of the seven hills surrounding Rome. Romulus killed Remus in an argument and Romulus' village became the city of Rome.

Household Numina

The early Roman religion was based on a belief in invisible spirits, called numina. There was a numina for everything, including the home, mountain, lakes, the day, and the night. Each family had its own numina. The numina Vesta ruled over the hearth fire. Lares was the numina who guarded the home and farm. The penates were gods of the pantry where food was stored. Fathers, or paterfamilias, prayed to the gods on behalf of their wives, children, and slaves.

From Greek to Roman

Historians believe the Etruscans taught the Romans to worship gods whose works could be seen, such as the god of the hearth, and to make statues of them. The Etruscans were believed to have introduced the Greek gods and goddesses to the Romans. When Romans adopted Greek gods, they changed the names. The Greek god Zeus became the Roman god Jupiter, who was the king of the **immortals** and ruled the sky. Aphrodite became Venus, goddess of love. The Romans added more gods to this group of many gods, called a pantheon. They also adopted the gods of the people they conquered or traded with. Romans worshiped the Egyptian goddess Isis. In Egypt, Isis was the goddess of nature. In Rome, Isis became a mother goddess and many temples were dedicated to her. The Persian god Mithras was also worshiped by Romans in bloody ceremonies where bulls were sacrificed.

A bronze sculpture of a numina

The Pantheon is a temple dedicated to the Roman gods.

MAGRIPPALFCOSTERTIVMFECIT

The Gods and Goddesses

The pantheon was the entire family of gods, each playing a different role in the lives of human beings. These gods were human in form and emotion and they had human adventures. Romans made a deal with their gods—if the gods did something for the Romans, the Romans would do something for them. Roman generals gave offerings to Mars, god of war, in hopes of winning battles. Young brides made offerings to Juno, the goddess of women and marriage, when they wanted to have healthy babies.

The sacred fire of Vesta was enclosed in a round temple in Rome. The fire of Vesta was never permitted to go out, for fear that terrible evil would come to Rome and its citizens. A vestal was a girl from a powerful family, chosen between the ages of six and ten, who promised to guard the fire for 30 years. If she broke her promise by marrying, she was buried alive in an underground chamber.

Power of the Gods

Romans prayed to please the gods, who could cause storms at sea, withhold the rains, or make sure a hunt was successful. They were afraid of angering the gods through their words or actions, so they took care to build temples for them and to hold elaborate annual festivals in their honor, such as the Saturnalia held in December. At this carnival, slaves were free for the day and their masters served them, instead of the other way around.

Spread of Christianity

By 100 A.D., a new religion called Christianity spread through the empire. Christianity followed the teachings of Jesus Christ. Jesus lived in the Roman province of Palestine and was put to death by its governor, Pontius Pilate, around 30 A.D. Christianity's followers, or Christians, believed Jesus was the son of God. They refused to worship Roman gods. The Romans believed Christianity was dangerous and a threat to the empire. For nearly 200 years, Christians were imprisoned, tortured, or killed by the Romans. Some emperors tried to destroy Christianity by burning churches and outlawing its worship. The more Christians that were killed, or martyred, the faster the religion seemed to grow. In 313 A.D., Roman Emperor Constantine converted, or changed his religion, to Christianity after having a vision on a battlefield. Almost 70 years later, the Emperor Theodosius made Christianity the official religion of the Roman Empire.

Venus: Goddess of Fields and Gardens

Venus was a Roman goddess and daughter of Jupiter, king of the gods. The Romans adopted her from the Greek goddess Aphrodite, the goddess of love and beauty. Venus became a goddess of fields and gardens and the wife of Vulcan, god of fire. Charming and radiant, she had many children, including Cupid. Romans gave Venus' name to the planet Venus.

Mercury: God of Merchants

Mercury, the Roman god of merchants, was often depicted holding a purse because he was thought to help people in business. Mercury wore winged sandals or a winged hat to help speed him on his errands. The Romans honored him with a festival held on May 15. Named after the fast-moving Roman god, the planet Mercury orbits the sun more quickly than any other planet.

Ancient Japan

Japan is made up of a chain of volcanic islands in the Pacific Ocean, 120 miles (200 km) from the east coast of China. The ancient Japanese worshiped gods and goddesses of nature as well as ancestor spirits. Over time, their beliefs evolved into a religion called Shinto. As new peoples settled in Japan, they brought their own faiths and customs and these too spread throughout Japan.

300 B.C.–1582 A.D.

Shinto

Shinto, which means "the way of the gods," was the first religion practiced in Japan. Shinto combined a love of nature with the worship of ancestor spirits, known as *kami*. Shintoists believed that when someone died, his or her spirit lived on as a *kami*. *Kami* were believed to control events, such as the outbreak of disease, when they were angered or ignored. People left gifts of food and drink at small shrines in their homes to honor and please the *kami*. Shinto has no official scriptures or rules. Followers of Shinto believed that a person's actions were judged as good or bad depending on their intentions.

Shinto Shrines

The ancient Japanese built Shinto shrines in natural settings. Shintoists believed that *kami* lived in nature, so the shrines were built next to waterfalls and rocks and in caves and forest clearings. People visited the shrines to pray for good luck, to thank the *kami* for their blessings, and to **reflect**. Most shrines had a garden, a worship hall, and a *kami* hall for the *kami* to live. A mirror, jade stone, or sword hung on the wall facing the *kami* hall as a symbol of the *kami*'s presence. Before entering, visitors washed their hands and mouths in a fountain. Shintoists believed that cleanliness was necessary for a person to be in a peaceful state of mind for prayer.

Kami Cats

An ancient Japanese myth tells of an emperor traveling in a rainstorm one evening. A cat sitting in a doorway waved to him as he passed. The emperor got off his horse and walked toward the cat. When he reached it, a bolt of lightning struck and killed his horse. The emperor believed the cat was a *kami* and had protected him. To this day, many Japanese believe that cats are helpful *kami*.

According to the Kojiki, *a record of ancient Japanese mythology and history, Earth was once just a watery mass. The god Izanagi and the goddess Izanami stirred the waters with a long, jeweled spear. The water that dripped from the spear when it was pulled out, thickened and became the island of Onokoro. Izanagi and Izanami lived on the island and had many children. The legend states that some of the children turned into the islands of Japan.*

Confucianism

Confucius was a Chinese scholar who lived from 551 B.C. to 479 B.C. Confucius stated that it was important for people to behave in a dutiful way to their families and society. This meant that a ruler must be kind to his subjects; a father must be kind to his children; a husband must be kind to his wife; an older brother must be kind to his younger brother; and an older friend must be kind to a younger friend. Ancient Japanese adopted Confucianism and modeled their public and family lives on these rules, which were called the Five Right Relationships.

Buddhism

The religion of Buddhism began in India in 528 B.C. Buddhism eventually spread through Asia and China and was brought to Japan by a visiting Buddhist monk in 552 A.D. Later, rulers sent students, scholars, and monks to China to study Buddhism. Buddhists built temples for worship throughout the countryside. Over time, followers of Shinto adopted some Buddhist beliefs.

Burning the Dead

Buddhists believed that death was unclean, so they cremated, or burned, their dead. When Buddhism arrived in Japan, people began to practice cremation. After a body was cremated, relatives of the dead lifted a piece of bone from the ashes and placed it in a white pottery jar as a symbol that they had not abandoned the body. A funeral ceremony was held over the next 49 days, after which the bone was buried in a cemetery.

Jomon Pit Burials

About 10,000 years ago, a culture called Jomon developed on the island of Honshu. The Jomon peoples buried their dead in small pits. The body was laid out with its knees bent up and a stone was placed against its chest. Clay figures of women, such as the one shown right, which are believed to be fertility goddesses, were sometimes laid around the body.

Yayoi Group Graves

The Yayoi people buried their dead in large clay urns or heavy stone coffins. Graves were grouped together and marked with a heap of earth or a circle of stones. Rulers' graves were surrounded by a ditch to separate them from the commoners' graves. Possessions such as swords, beads, and mirrors were placed inside the ruler's coffin, so they could be used in the afterlife.

Yamato Mound Burials

Members of ruling families of the Yamato clan were buried in huge mounds of earth, called *kofun*. Later, *kofun* were keyhole-shaped. The dead person was placed in a small room in the mound, along with iron swords, arrowheads, tools, armor, and bracelets that the dead would need in the afterlife. Thousands of clay statues of humans, animals, and buildings were placed on top of the *kofun*. These statues are called *haniwa*. Historians do not know why they were put on graves.

Ancient Fortune-telling

The ancient Japanese believed that there were good and bad times for performing certain actions, such as going to war. Fortune-telling, or divination, was used to find out when the best time to act was. The most common method was to write a question, such as what the next season's weather or outcome of crops would be like, on a turtle shell or a cow's shoulder blade bone. Then the bone was heated until it cracked. A diviner studied the shape of the crack, then interpreted it as either a positive or negative answer to the question.

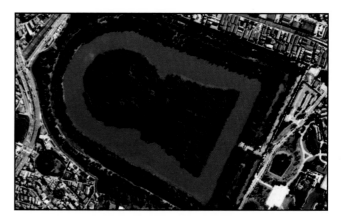

The keyhole-shaped Daisen Kofun is the largest kofun. *It is said to be the tomb for the Emperor Nintoku.*

Ancient Celts

Looking for more land to live on and farm, the ancient Celts spread out from present-day Austria and settled across Europe in 400 B.C. The Celts believed that different gods controlled all aspects of life on Earth. Many gods and goddesses were thought to live in and near water. Celts made sacrifices to the deities to gain their help and approval.

800 B.C.– 43 A.D.

Animal Gods

Most of the gods worshiped by the early Celts were animal spirits. The Celts made metal and wooden figurines of horses, boars, and bulls that were offered to the gods as votives. After trade with Greece and other nations increased, the Celts began to worship statues of gods and goddesses that had human bodies, as did the Greeks and the Romans. Most of these Celtic gods still had some animal features, such as the god Cernunnos, who was always depicted with horns.

Cernunnos

Sanctuaries and Sacrifices

The Celts worshiped their gods in forests by springs, rivers, and lakes, or at shrines and in sanctuaries. Sanctuaries were rectangular or circular buildings constructed in woodlands by water, or in the cities. Artisans worked at the sanctuaries in the cities, making gold and silver coins and decorated swords for visitors to toss into the sanctuary. Ditches and palisades surrounded the sanctuaries as a defense against raiders. Inside the sanctuaries, live animals, most often horses, were thrown into pits as offerings to the gods. People were sometimes sacrificed at the sanctuaries as well. Many Celtic sanctuaries, or holy places, contained the skulls of enemies which the Celts offered to the gods.

The goddess Epona was the protector of horses and riders. She was often shown as a woman sitting sideways on a mare.

Spiritual Leaders

Druids were the spiritual leaders of the Celtic community. Acting as priests, teachers, and doctors, they were considered the most important people in the community. At least one druid lived in each community. Versed in Celtic histories and knowledge, druids performed religious ceremonies, offered sacrifices to Celtic gods, and educated the children of nobles. The druids also created laws that described how to behave, and acted as judges when someone was accused of a crime. They also predicted the future by observing signs, called omens, in nature. This practice is called divination.

The wheel of the chariot was an important Celtic symbol, and was often depicted on Celtic coins.

The Otherworld

The Celts believed that after death, a person's spirit went to the Otherworld, where spirits lived before they were born and after they died. In the Otherworld, warriors attended feasts at which cauldrons of beer and mead never emptied and animals were made whole again after being eaten. Some Celts believed that people could visit the Otherworld while still alive by finding secret, hidden passages in nature.

Celebrating the Seasons

The Celts celebrated each season with a religious festival of feasting, games, and sacrifices to the gods. The start of spring was celebrated on February 1, at the Imbolc feast, which was a **pastoral** festival. The Celts held the festival of Beltane on May 1, to celebrate summer. Druids herded cattle between two bonfires as a ritual to keep them healthy, and houses were decorated with greenery to welcome fertility to farms. The Feast of Lugnasad celebrated fall. The festival began on August 1, and lasted for a month. Samain, held on October 31, celebrated the start of winter. Samain was the most important festival because it was believed that the powers of the Otherworld were let loose on Earth. Human and animal sacrifices were made to please the gods of the Otherworld.

Burial Mounds

Kings, chieftains, and nobles were buried in enormous mounds of earth. Each mound had one or more wooden burial chambers inside it. Items that the Celts believed the dead person needed in the Otherworld were laid around the body. Warriors' burial chambers were filled with spears, swords, and shields. The graves of kings and queens contained chariots, silk cloth, and amber and glass beads. Working people were cremated or buried in simple graves with small offerings, such as brooches.

Votives, or presents, were placed in the graves of dead Celts as offerings to the gods of the Otherworld. Many votives, such as this man in a boat, were carved from wood. The Celts believed that trees, especially oak trees, were sacred bridges between the people on Earth and the gods in the sky.

Celtic Christians

The end of Celtic dominance in Europe arrived when Julius Caesar, a Roman general, conquered most of their lands, beginning around 58 B.C. The Romans eventually defeated the Celts in France and England. They never managed to conquer the Celts in the highlands of Scotland or in Ireland. The Celtic culture in Ireland remained intact well into the 400s A.D. when Christianity was introduced to the Celts. Many Celts converted to Christianity, but adapted some of their way of life into their new religious beliefs. For example, hundreds of stone crosses were raised in Ireland and Scotland by Celtic Christians. The crosses combined a circle, the Celtic symbol for the moon, and the Christian cross.

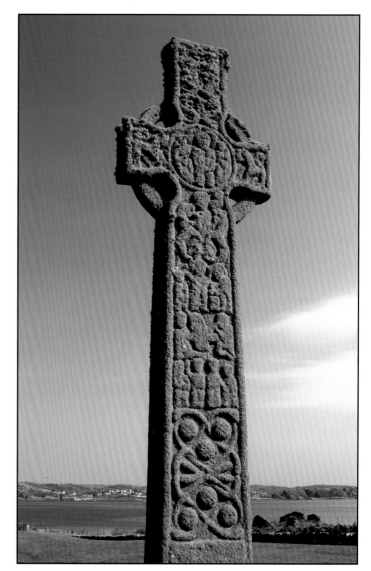

Celtic crosses are made from granite and stone, and stand at monasteries, castles, and churches throughout Ireland and Scotland.

Ancient Vikings

The early Vikings, who lived in the region of Scandinavia, worshiped a number of gods and goddesses and believed in an afterlife where great warriors were rewarded. As the Vikings settled in new lands across Europe, they began to accept the beliefs of other peoples.

787 A.D.–1100 A.D.

Nine Worlds

Vikings believed that the world of humans, which they called Midgard, or Middle Earth, was only one of nine worlds. The other worlds included Asgard, the home of the gods; Hel, the place of the dead; and Jotunheim, the land of the frost giants. Each world was believed to be at a different height on the trunk of a great ash tree, named Yggdrasil, which stretched up through the universe.

Gods and Goddesses

Odin was the Vikings' supreme god of wisdom and warfare. The most popular god was Thor, the thunder god. He was believed to have worn a magic belt made by dwarves that gave him incredible strength, and to have hit giants with his hammer, without ever missing his mark. The most important female god was Freya, who was the goddess of love and fertility.

Ragnarok

The Vikings believed that the end of the world would be caused by a severe ice age that would destroy human civilization. Odin would then lead the gods of Asgard in a final battle called Ragnarok, against the giants, led by the mischievous god, Loki. This fierce battle would destroy the universe, and the surviving gods would rule a new world.

Life in Valhalla

Vikings believed in an afterlife. The souls of most people were thought to go to Hel, a place like Earth, where they would stay until Ragnarok. Evil people became ghosts, while warriors who died in battle were taken to Valhalla, Odin's hall. In Valhalla, warriors ate well, drank as much mead as they wanted, and practiced for war so that they could help the gods battle Loki and the giants at Ragnarok. Valhalla was believed to have more than 500 doors to accommodate all the Viking warriors who arrived after dying in battle.

Odin was the ruler of the gods. He gave up one of his eyes in exchange for wisdom.

Funeral Ships

The Vikings buried their dead in ships as a symbol of the journey that the soul makes to the next world. Chieftains and warriors were often buried in large wooden ships called longships filled with items for the afterlife, such as weapons, clothing, jewelry, and horses. Ordinary people were buried in smaller boats and had fewer items buried with them. Sometimes a ship was burned, and its ashes buried in the belief that the dead person's spirit would be carried to the next world more quickly. Today, the burning of a model of a Viking ship has become a custom during *Hogmanay*, or New Year, celebrations in Scotland.

The Coming of Christianity

The Vikings first encountered Christianity when they settled in Ireland, France, and England. The Viking settlers there became Christians in about 900 A.D. By 1100 A.D., Iceland and the Scandinavian countries had converted to Christianity, and Christianity was made the official religion of the Vikings. The Vikings began to live more peaceful lives. Eventually they married into local families and took on the ways of the local cultures.

Even after becoming Christians, the Vikings did not abandon their beliefs in Norse gods. Amulets and gravestones often depicted both Christian and Norse symbols. Today the old Viking religion of many gods and goddesses is still one of several official religions in Iceland, where it is known as *Asatru*.

Large stones were placed around Viking graves in the shape of a boat.

The Vikings buried their dead in funeral ships with items to be used in the afterlife.

Viking Artifacts

The best-preserved Viking remains have been found at burial sites. These sites allow archaeologists to learn what life was like during the Viking Age. Inside a burial mound in Norway, archaeologists found a ship built around 900 A.D. that contained the body of a Viking chieftain or king. The skeleton wore wool and silk clothing and was lying on the remains of a wooden bed. Fish hooks, cups, wooden plates and mixing bowls, and a large cask for holding water were also found on the ship. The bodies of twelve horses and six dogs were laid around the boat. The Vikings believed the chieftain would use all of these items in the afterlife.

Glossary

altar A platform used in religious ceremonies

ancestor A person from whom one is descended

brahman An ancient Indian priest of the highest social level

city-state An independent city, usually walled for defense, and the surrounding towns and villages that depend upon it for defense

cuneiform A form of writing invented by the Sumerians in which words or ideas were represented by characters

deity A god or goddess

descend Relating to a certain family or group

embalmer A person who prevents decay of dead bodies by treating them with preservatives before burying them

empire A political unit that occupies a large region of land and is governed by one ruler

famine A great shortage of food that causes widespread hunger and starvation

fertility The ability to produce life

guru A great teacher

immortal Those who do not die; the gods

meditate The act of thinking quietly

mortar A building material used to bind stone together

mythology The collection of stories having to do with gods and goddesses

omens Signs of good or bad things to come

pastoral Relating to the country or country life

patron Someone who supports or protects a city, nation, or people

prophecy A message that tells the wishes of a god or predicts the future

reflect To think about one's life or experiences

sacred Having special religious meaning

sacrifice The act of killing an animal or person as an offering to a god in a religious ceremony

sanctuary A holy or sacred place

scribes People who make a living by copying or recording text

script Recorded language

Shinto The first religion practiced in Japan, which combined a love of nature with the worship of ancestor spirits

supernatural Beyond the usual powers of nature

Trojan War A ten-year war between the ancient Greeks and Trojans in which the city of Troy was destroyed

Index

Websites

www.bbc.co.uk/history/ancient/
 Amazing images highlight in-depth looks into ancient cultures.
www.historyforkids.org/
 This site provides information on the history, food, clothing, technology, stories, and religion of many ancient cultures.
www.pbs.org/wgbh/nova/ancient/
 Interactive videos take readers through ancient civilizations.
www.archaeolink.com/amazing_worlds_of_archaeology1.htm
 This site provides links to sites with archaeological information.

Further Reading

Ancient Art and Cultures series, Rosen Publishing Group 2010

Biography from Ancient Civilizations: Legends, Folklore, and Stories of Ancient Worlds series, Mitchell Lane Publishers 2009

Ancient Civilizations and Their Myths and Legends, Rosen Central 2009

Ancient and Medieval People series, Benchmark books 2009